WITHDRAWN
UTSA LIBRARIES

P9-ECJ-527

RENEWALS 691-4574

DATE DUE

JUL 13

Demco, Inc. 38-293

Green Dragons

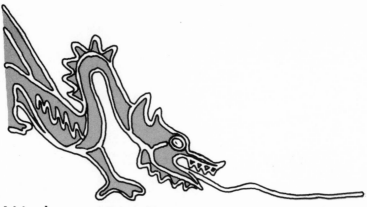

Wesleyan New Poets

Green Dragons

Richard Katrovas

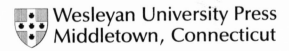

Wesleyan University Press
Middletown, Connecticut

Copyright © 1983 by Richard Katrovas
All rights reserved.

Acknowledgment is gratefully made to the following magazines, in the pages of
which many of these poems first appeared:
Antioch Review; *Berkeley Poetry Review*; *Black Warrior Review*; *Columbia*; *Crazy
Horse*; *INTRO 12*; *Mid-American Review*; *Missouri Review*; *New England Review*;
The New Virginia Review; *North American Review*; *Poetry East*; *Telescope*.

I would like to thank the University of Virginia for a Henry Hoyns fellowship year
during which many of these poems were written and rewritten. I would also like to
thank my teacher and friend Carolyn Forché for her unflagging support.

Thanks also to Barbara Cully, Glover Davis, Robert L. Jones, James Turner, James
Whitehead, and David Wojahn.

All inquiries and permissions requests should be addressed to the Publisher,
Wesleyan University Press, 110 Mt. Vernon Street, Middletown, Connecticut 06457
Distributed by Harper & Row Publishers, Keystone Industrial Park, Scranton,
Pennsylvania 18512
Manufactured in the United States of America
First Edition

ISBN   0-8195-2114-0   Cloth
ISBN   0-8195-1115-3   Paper

LIBRARY
The University of Texas
At San Antonio

For Betty
　　My Egypt
　　and Mom & Dad Johnson,
　　　　who took me in

```
━━━  ━━
━━━  ━━
━━━━━━━  Chên
━━  ━━
━━  ━━
━━━━━━
```

The Arousing is thunder, the dragon.
It is dark yellow, it is a spreading
out, a great road, the eldest son.
It is decisive and vehement; it is
bamboo that is green and young.

The Book of Changes

The existence of what I truly love is felt
by me as a necessity, a need without which
my life cannot be satisfied, fulfilled,
complete.

Karl Marx

Contents

I

II

6

III

IV

I

Bloomfield, Inc.

My little ones pull
from the ground, hands
cupping their faces like petals,
like shields. Thus they go
wandering, not so blindly
as aimlessly, under several stars,
bumping, turning, robed
in gauze-white gowns.
That is my dream.
In this life, rooted
in the mercy of the State,
they are the flowers of the Commonwealth.
Peroxide, urine, Betadine, Unisalve:
the several scents comprising
a single scent that will not wash
from my skin. The coins
I am given to care for them
are diminished in their eyes.
I look into their eyes.
What do they see in my eyes?
Nothing gauche as pity.
I cannot wipe their asses,
lift them in and out of bed
and pity them.
Not for minimum wage.
Harry, seventeen,
sixty-four-pound quadraplegic,
my *Mr. Nonsequitur*, what do you *mean*
I'm a bad angel in God's air force?
What do you *mean* I aint seen
pussy since pussy seen me?

When I pull the morning shift
I lift you from the sheets—
your eyes still closed, your
gorged penis pointing to Heaven—
Little friend, when you die
I won't weep. I won't even
get drunk. I'll drive
real fast on Rt. 29
and if a full moon's up
I'll cut the lights. Home,
I'll read John Clare's
"I Am" and later on
burst out laughing in the dark.
Harry, some of us are real slow.
Some of us will never get it.
Now, I gather what I can and cannot
hold. The earth's burnt fingers
I hold to my lips and coo into them.
My dreams are prophylactic, small, and soiled.
In one there is a door I kick and kick.
My arms spilling flowers from the field.
Richard, I say, *Richard, let me in.*

Drink

The dancers have gone home.
Outside. Low tide. Five A.M.
What moves moves slowly,
even lovers under blankets
in the cool sand. I wrap
my fingers in a towel,
swirl another glass.
Through the picture window
I watch ringed fires
falling into ash. What burned
all night will burn again:
Sweet Billy Hammer,
white boy with the bushy 'fro,
leader of the hottest
band in town, squats
in the blue footlights
flying through licks
on his Martin with the amp off.
I empty the rubber spill-
catcher into a brandy snifter
and top it off with house
sour mash. Taking it to him,
I'll not say, Billy, these
are the night's dregs, drink
and your hands will grow dark,
a moon will rise in your palm
and you will pinch it and strum
a song no one can dance to. . . .
His eyes shut tight,
he is healing, privately,
and would not hear me.

He has never burdened me with his story,
nor I him with mine,
for this we are grateful to each other
and are quiet like the truly grateful.
The stunned shadows of morning's fringe
penetrate the powdered light he inhabits.
I stand before him
waiting for a sign, a break.
He plays on, and on
the third finger of his left hand
a gold band triggers slips of light,
sixteenth notes dissolving into others.
Do you play this song for her, Billy?
Is your heart burning,
or is it simply something cool that glows?
Who cares. The dogs are catching
fire on the beach-front porches.
Joggers grunt by in their grey
sweatsuits and miles away
a siren blasts
and peters out. This smear
of paradise is plugging
into sunshine. Drink,
tip this glass I bring you
and drain it without breathing.

The Disenfranchised

From the rear window
where he slept the stars
were mouths of angels
opened he could see their song.
The smell of piss
and the younger ones
below on the seat
breathing audibly

we saw too much we
suffered our father's leather
every hundred miles we
ate sometimes not for days we
did not love one another.
In the beginning just me
and my brother then the small
ones came. This is no
easy story to tell those

who lived in the other America.
He asked his mother
What's a merica?
She folded her hands
over her swollen belly
"Just a word the Republic
of Burma Shave." *When she talked*
like that I shut up. She was
beautiful enough to be a star
he thought she could even sing
on television. When things

got scary on the snow-clogged
mountain roads with no chains
and many tongues clamoring
through the static she said
their angel would take care
of them. She said he lived
in the trunk. She said
he made himself small or large.
When the car spun wheels
and swerved she said he swelled
and wrapped us. In the desert
he swelled and wrapped the hot engine.
In cities where the bad police
were everywhere he made them
invisible. Seven years they were
invisible in America then their
angel died. *I dreamed in a Holiday Inn*
I walked outside under pink
sky the trunk snapped open
he lay curled all white
and naked a faint yellow light
pouring from his parted lips.

Things quickened. They took
to hocking spare tires and stealing
outright. *Once a fat hamburger maker*
chased our father and jumped on his back.
The white bag of food fell in the snow
and their father punched him so hard
he fell and didn't move.

We cried and ate our burgers.
The rest is history.
The rest is bullshit.

When I remember them now
those two beautiful stupid
young people and their five kids
living in a car
running from the cops
across a more affluent America
than will ever be again
when I remember the years
he spent in prison and the years
she spent waiting on Welfare for him
when I remember crawling in bed with her
and wanting to be him for her
and not understanding what that meant
I tense my body at the knowledge
that what I remember has nothing to do
with how it was. The disenfranchised
of America propagate
and a few of their numbers join the ranks
of the hysterical proud ruling body.
They become dangerous to their own kind
and take up campaigning for issues.
There are no issues.
There is only the body with its list of needs
and the tuning fork in the spine
that swells the skull
when we have died past weeping.

Green Dragons   Wet Feathers

Now, gods, stand up for bastards!

Edmund (*King Lear*)

Seven years since last he phoned
from this same cheap motel.
I'll get drunk with him
and that will affirm something.
I am stationed in the same chair
and he assumes the same other
chair at the opposite end
of the room. The sign outside
blinks *Seven Seas Seven*
Seas and he studies me.
In this manner we share
a kind of trance. Cubes
pop in our glasses as the auburn
liquid dilutes into evening
when it is the glow of his cigarette
I watch arching from lips
to lap and only after
this eerie hour of speechlessness
would I bring myself
to say if I could speak

Father stand up and open
your arms so I may run to you
and hold you so tightly
your spine cracks. On the broadway
green dragons ride drunk

17

sailors' arms and another
woman is planted in the violet
shrubs of Horton Plaza.
As crumbs sprinkle the pavement
from a bum's French loaf
so sons are scattered
from the flesh and Father
I consume myself
just to get back to you.
Stand up you beautiful
half-dead bastard
and let me hold myself and cry

In the gauze light of false dawn
a boy pulls a chiffon dress
over his head. Smoking
long brown cigarettes
he will wait into morning
with his legs crossed
for a general to come
and hold a hanky
of ice to sores
on his shoulder blades.
He will clinch his head
between his knees
and let the old soldier
push a straightened paper clip
into the pink
translucent blisters
releasing holy water
then the first

wet feathers. On the other
edge of light a professor
rips all his diplo-
mas to shreds.
In the privacy of his office
half-lotus in the dark
he dips a plastic straw
into the void and takes

a long draw. So all
our little fathers help
us come to nothing
give us wings and secrets
and magic lanterns
give us gaits and swaggers
and tunes to whistle

at the stars . . . Stand up
Father stand up and proselytize.
Put your hands on the chair arms
lean forward shift weight
to your feet rise up
and keep going up through
the ceiling past fields
of aerials into the crowded

city sky. Then for chrisake
say something   anything
with authority. Tell me
of shadows wearing badges

and the rat on a wheel
in your testicles. Tell me
motherfucker's a prison mantra
and there's no place like home.

Father, I am the ink
of your loins
an indelible angel
puffed and throbbing.
Tell me skin is not worthy
of ink and ink not worthy
of mythic design.

Father, I Know

that I have changed,
you have changed,
and the spoiled meat
that is my love for you
sways on hooks in a chilled room
of a woman's life

that there is no weather
in Hell, only the occasional
sultry voice
of a bureaucrat
shifting like breezes
the fine dust covering everything

that from the Book of Stars
we read *no death just*
fall to your knees
and weep and man
to man means swing
your balls in time
with your father,
his father, his father

that long ago a man
and a woman dragged their shadows
from a cave and were blinded
by possibilities, one
of which was to hold
their breaths
till they saw stars

that in every stinking closet
a platoon of nightmares
is maneuvering

that from Good Deals
we inherit a legacy of sorrow,
that your children got a good deal,
that with the pebbles
in your shoes you
made a little mound
somewhere isolated and forlorn

that in the *Book of Changes*
there is no hexagram
for the unborn,
for they are divine
and merciless and flock
together onto lakes
that are our eyes
when we are
looking back.

The Windows of Your Room

for Joan

How many men, in dreams, have lain with their mothers?
No reasonable man is troubled by such things.

Iokaste (*Oedipus Rex*)

I

I gathered potatoes that fell from trains
and brought them home to you in burlap sacks.
What is it called when that which is given
is given back like rain on the ocean?
The stains in your sheets that never came out—
drippings from sunsets you held inside you
or the maps of those continents of pain
you traveled and charted alone at night?
How could all his letters full of nothing
make sense, woman, of all your wasted days?
Dogs barked. The whole horizon flared and turned
its back to you while I was sleeping.
The windows of your room were black mirrors
the pale bulb shone within like something caught
and fixed forever in the final stage of birth.
How could you dream so much beyond this life?
How could you sing while peeling potatoes?
As a blue freight train passes through my sleep
it ejects a red feather that will float
always between you and my memory
of what you had been and what you became

as the duration of his absences
tapped louder and louder at your windows.

II

Smelling of its new rain, Merrimac Street
ticked and steamed, runoff flowing with leaves
and trash into the sewers of the town.
Racing sticks and splashing in the swollen
gutters, with no shadows to tell time by,
each of us held a June bug by a string,
tasted our own bodies' salt, and screamed, laughed
in that vague season you took to crawling
and spoke, seriously, with things broken.
The light in your room stayed on every night;
the yellow outline of your door still seals
dark corridors that have no genesis.

III

You breathe on the window, spiral the fog
with a fingertip and sip your coffee.
You spot an angel with brown teeth laughing
in the wintered branches of the dogwood
and know the morning's off to a bad start.
Perhaps the mailman will be late again
and I will come home for lunch completely
naked, this time having lost everything,
or the social worker will come to stay,

her Samsonite packed with clipboards and pens.
So your hands drift to your breasts and linger.

IV

Who has drunk from this foul water?
The polished street on which the autos slide
and the drunk old man hating its thin glow.
But they are partners, the street and the man;
they mutter together, forget their names,
and desire the bodies of children.
Howling from sleep for a world of sugar,
buckling shadows, firing the streetscape,
the dawn, the light received you trembling
and the street, the man, the ghosts of your pain
will glut, will sicken, will be gone by spring.

V

The glitter of wet on the first morning.
A shape in the far corner of the world
the light is just coming to. A woman
holds in the pocket of her crouched body
a male child with no skin; and as the light
arrives, the shadow of her hanging breasts
is not enough, nor are tears, urine
or excrement enough to cool him off.
Quietly, she prepares the earth's first meal.

26

A Most Mysterious Woman

(Sasebo, Japan, 1967)

There are ashes in the belly
of a girl in Sasebo. She
breathes dusk into our lives
and a light breeze
accompanies her
into the American sector,
past minesweepers
rocking in their slips,
past the giant oiler
lolling in its song
of tamed fires and constant smoke,
past the silver hangars
where men will work into her night
not singing, not even humming.
Pausing at the quay wall
I regard
an actual red sun
extinguishing
99 Islands off Kiushu,
and remain to behold
the coming on of each star
across the broadening dark.
The flurry carries my vision
to the southern peak of Mt. Oboshi
and continues one, and one,
and another, until the facing slope
is littered with stars.
I know they are the lanterns

of those who have come
from the north, the students
who will scatter
bilingual leaflets
saying the *Enterprise*
is killing fish,
the students who will snake
5 thousand strong 3 miles
through the city
past skivvy girls dripping
out of bars, past sailors
staring into benjo ditches, past
squid vendors and pachinko parlors,
stopping at the ancient
stone bridge leading
to the base. There,
they will throw themselves
in waves against the blue wall
of riot squad, and many will fall
upon the shallow water's rocks,
disturbing the gentle floating
Sakura petals and green
drifting moss. I light
the twentieth or thirtieth
cigarette I have ever smoked
and forget in this darkness
how ripe my face has become,
how I must each morning
cake on the skin-toned placebo
before the mirror
and slick back my hair

so the sorry sideburns
will show. Right here,
right now, the essence
of a most mysterious woman
is the very air I'm breathing,
and no one will know this night
I am loosing a smear
of dream into her lapping water.

Ekura Deska?

You said my lips
were like a woman's, that
you could make me up
into a yankee sister
and fool those bastard sailor
boys. I said with the words
you had taught me
Where is your heart, Suki,
and you moved my fingers
to your lips and fell
to your knees. I'd have said
Ekura deska? but I knew
what it cost, the flat rate
for a mouth such as yours,
though for me it cost nothing.
I was your *skivvy boy-san*
who followed you into alley
houses men had not seen,
where women passed
their days humming
the old songs to half-breed
infants: sitting lotus
on the worn tatami floors,
nursing and reading.
Today, I gather the bones
of a tropical winter,
the tiny shells I will string
and wear and perhaps
on some future date pass on
to a woman as token.
She might, on some good

summer evening further on,
a little giddy with palm
breezes and strong salt air,
latch them around the neck
of another man. And so on.
Suki, your silhouette through
rice paper squatting to a bowl
of soapy water . . . I waited
in the foyer cursing the hands
that bruised you. He would
go away with nothing of you
but your odor and that would fade.
You would come with me
out into streetlight
and we would walk,
mute and frazzled,
in yet another country
of the senses.

The Key

There is a lock in the light
we'll never turn, Louella,
there is no escaping what
we've seen. Your husband's
back swelled into a screen
on which his nightmare
played for you nightly:
the Vietnamese girl running
for his truck, explosives
strapped to her chest;
the order to shoot. Childless
after three years of marriage
to him you came to me
and came to me. I am reminded
of my numb thighs
under yours
when I was eighteen
and afraid to move and wake you.
I am reminded of the long calls
from that sad man, the walks
I took in winter streets
while you cried with him.
I am reminded of the letters
you received from your father
blasting you in the name of Christ.
I am reminded on nights such as these,
full of dark prospects and starrier than most.

Our Island

Our father's ship
has entered the mist.
His charmed cargo
will grow precious in the hold
but will never spoil,
salted, as it is, by tears.
He's charted a course
for the birthmark
you have on your back,
I in miniature on my forearm.
Once, dripping from the shower,
laughing, drunk and steaming
in the cold motel room,
he stretched the blue-veined skin
of his scrotum into a map
and showed us the same marking.
I wish him safe passage.
I hope you do, too, Theresa Rene.
I wish him safe passage
from this world of banks and prisons
so he may haul his cargo of outrageous needs
into his own blood and search always
for our island. May he be a hero
unto himself and may you
never forget,
that though I do not know
the woman you've become
you were my first lover
lying upside down next to me
so we could tickle each other's feet.
Come here, turn over, I'd whisper,

and in the dirty light from street lamps
illuminating our room,
I traced with my best finger
over and over
the coastline of your island
till you slept.

The Court of Two Sisters

*It is said the two sisters favored Shrimp Toulouse
and Crabmeat Rector. Their cook would always
prepare the two dishes the same evening so that
the sisters might partake of both on the same plate.
We invite you to do the same.*

The menu

Some night soon I'll pluck
the one good eye of God
and smear it
on these mossy walls
Annie, walk from this tourist trap
leaving my tips on the unbused tables.
Finding you
in one or another
French Quarter women's bar
I'll buy us drinks till I'm broke
because Annie
any kind of work is work
is work and we wash our hands
at the close of each night's take
like holy flies
that strut the walls of this courtyard,
their green backs
luminous in the green floodlight.
Every woman's sister, mother,
virgin aunt crawls off
under a butch moon
and her sons kiss

in the rouge glimmerings
of false awakenings
and Annie, when I am so drunk
with you I cannot stand
or sit or lie nodding
in the mellow stench
of my own free lunch
I'll fall into your small strong arms
and moan, baby.

Elegy for My Mother

Eleven years ago I left for good.
The earth has not cracked, nor the moon come down
to settle in among the lucid dead.
The fire in your vault drowns out the sound

of the gentle, screwing motion of the world.
Pitiful nights when caffeine wrecks my nerves
and I waver in the zone where murdered
children sing, I wonder if that flame deserves

anything as sumptuous as your body.
From harm to harm, the nights link day to day,
and women pass through my life like water
washing my body's pent-up seeds away

and on that flowing forth from dark to dark
I navigate according to no star.
I strike a match and watch it burn, finding
in its one act of mercy what we are.

Leaving the French Quarter

Old buildings breathe shadows
and noise of celebration rises
from these narrow streets.
Dusted with the glow
from second-story windows
your face glides next to me
as if your body were submerged.
It is the thickness of the air
I am considering, how our voices
are heavier, all light deeper,
as though the sun's ghost
were spreading out,
becoming this night's breath.
In Jackson Square, in the shadow
of the bronze horse, holding you,
I exhale my father
and for a moment we are two women crying.
Colored barlight soaks your hair and skin
and I think what I would not give
for the darkness of our hallway
where two bicycles rust together.
I hold your face, dumb and buzzing
trace the streaks of mascara
with a forefinger,
smudging this night on your cheek.
And as the hand from which suns rise
is opening, sky fades grey
and the statue ticks with the day's first rain,
we find shelter and know this storm
to be a summer thing, that when
it passes streets will glisten
for an hour more.

Glowing

I walked the beach all night
smoking cigarette after cigarette
thinking that as paper
burning down to ash
is a kind of great release,
so would I give up the substance of remembrance
to dawn at the cliffs in autumn,
to the purple coming on
and eventual bursting forth of light
in the face of real scenery.
I wanted to kill the voices,
pinch the vortex at the tip
where it entered me
and flip it inside out; that is,
be the scenery, the light that makes it real
and the silence that is the border
between light and all light enters.
I wanted to leave and come back
as something sexless and wise;
I wanted to love myself so much
nothing else mattered.
I did not care that everything—
the sand, the water, the cool air
and its mixed odors—would come with me.
I had embarked,
a solitary head of hair
and cursed eyes
fixed in a starless night
on the very dark that consumed me,
and if the world wanted to follow
I didn't care. I wouldn't look back.

Yet such is the small care
with which we burden the act of going forth
and such is the song
that is a kind of soap
to soften the heart
when it has turned to leather.
Such is the sound of sand
blown against glass
and the hissing of the soul
as it travels through the primary colors
and emerges in the dark; say, the dark room
of a former lover, or a lover
you'll someday enter like a worm
and eat yourself out of,
or the lover waiting for you,
now, in his or her
own black rags of yearning and denial.
Yes, all fly in a centrifuge of denial
and their names are residue
you'll scrape off and work
into the pores of your face
and yes your face will glow in the dark
and that's the point
you are only a face glowing in the dark.

Crimes

Four years ago, when you were *coming out*,
I stood one morning in Jackson Square
and pleaded with the God of Pure Motives
to send a cleansing rain. The clockwork showers
of early summer came only and I sliced a path
through that ordinary thunder
and my punk heart found the watermark
of its mercy. You did not know then
I regarded you as the other half
of something only a woman could love.
Friend, I cannot say I've touched you
through her or that I may ever touch you.
What moves in her moves me
and what moves in me moves nothing.
What moves in you is the heart of this city
and she is the heart of this city.
That over the years, after nights of dancing,
you've held each other and slept with your clothes on
frightens me. Such love is a mystery
and I am a fool for mystery.

In the neuter, pale hour
of the redoubling footfall,
when he who has never danced
awakens in Exchange Alley,
his brain crisp and flaking,
any woman, girl or boy
is ground to powder.
That I would kill that man,
press my thumbs to his throat
till he changed to the color

43

of a dawn sky, is another kind of mystery.
I would then gather the limp hulk
into my arms and waltz it to Lake Pontchartrain.
I would then lie down with it on the muddy bank,
fold its head into the crook of my arm,
stroke the greasy hair, and sleep.

Our most passionate crimes are perpetrated in Heaven,
and the last morning stars are vigilantes that will return.

After four years I return,
and when she is not drunk past dreaming
the only woman I've ever held all night
bolts upright, gasping.
The nightmare is not altered in the dream.
You, when no other man could touch her,
touched her. Danced her into exhaustion
so she could sleep. I shall take you in my arms,
Brother, Sister to my lover, and there will be no mystery.

The Mystic Pig

On the balcony of *La Fitte in Exile*,
on the corner of Bourbon and Dumaine,
at the intersection of the Merciful
Embrace and the Middle Finger, where Hope's punk,
Desire, taps his cane along the cracked sidewalk,
where I, awed, disgusted, yet wholly
reconciled must pass each night never daring
to gaze up, the Boys of Summer are doing
the Mystic Pig. It seems they are not always
gentle with one another. It seems they
are forever beating their wings yet never
taking off. In this city, where the mauve
resonance of a summer dusk is just
another flag announcing predilection,
these sons have found sanctuary. They will
go forth upon the packed avenues, seeking
love while shunning the rhetoric of love;
for they have learned to live in a new
language and it is terminal:

Blue flag right hip pocket—*I shall cradle
you for an hour and fill you up with your
father's shadow.*

Brown flag left hip pocket—*I shall humble
myself before you and receive your darkest
blessing.*

Red flag right hip pocket—*I shall salute you
as you sing your anthem of remorse . . .*

So the passions of men for men are beautifully
reduced, refined, bathed in the blood of the Mystic Pig.

How shall I go forth among these angels,
an interloper to their world,
to them a charter member
of the Brotherhood of Mother Fuckers?

I'll go quietly,
gazing neither up nor down
nor left nor right,
keeping their joy, their pain,
their mysterious nobility
on the slow-burning periphery.

God, It Is Like a Man

to want a woman more
when she is sleeping,
to rise from the bed
he shares with her
and stand in the dark
sex-scented air
of their room, smoking.
I splash Christian Brothers
Brandy into a paper cup
and tip the cheap heat
to my lips, beginning
the night's forfeiture
of memory. The penultimate
trolly soothes through fog
on Saint Charles Street.
The silhouettes in its yellow-
lighted windows pooled
their silence
and will bank it in the dawn.
A chill slips the length
of my spine and I think
that somewhere, someone
I loved for a night
is sharpening
this night on her wrist;
and somewhere else
someone like me is rolling
on asphalt, holding
his crotch. Right now
all of us are thinking
about You, Father of Glint,

Father of Dull, Father
of the shadow-eating
lights of cars. God,
what is it in me
that would crush the night-
blooming chakras
of a dreaming woman,
stick a finger
in her moist sleep
and frig her back
to this dark room and me . . .
God, I have not spoken
to you since I
was a boy and thought
you lay on the other
side of stars. At night
I begged you to reach
down and make a loose
fist around me. Now
I ask you to reach
down and make a loose
fist around my wife.

History of Breath

When I am out in the traffic of men,
Following a false lead
Or simply walking a dim street,
Some part of me wishes me otherwise;

Some part, some lucid measure given
By you, rendered by you as longing
Makes one into whom he longs for,
Though falsely, tenderly at least.

I go out and come back in like breath.
A life, any life, is little more than breath.
A worker's breath, or sleeper's, or lover's
Cadenced shaping of the air, giving, taking

Of the air, seems a history worth knowing.
The condensation of your breath
Upon my cheek when you are sleeping
And I am not would be the perfect page

For one average mind's illumination.
To shed a tear would clear the page
But this is what is perfect: that I go
Out, one hurting face among hurt faces,

One forced smile in a driven world
of obsequious sellers and fearful
Buyers, as a student from a class he'll fail
Again and again yet never stop taking,

Though knowing he may never master it,
Hoping still to be someday conversant in the history of breath.

IV

The Blue Candle

He presses his ear to cool plaster
and hears pipes hissing, women
talking, until a sigh scrapes
his spine and he is in their room
and they are dancing in water.
The smaller one pushes the other's
hand away but the hand drifts back.
Their shoulders touch and the border
of their skins is vague. They share
a cigarette, eat olives from a bowl.
On a table by their bed a candle
makes prisms of two empty wineglasses;
the colors quiver on the walls.
Shadows in the sheets wrap them, ripple
when they turn and find him naked,
squatting in the air above the floor.
His eyes flare back. Though he
has come for this he can't perform
the unmentionable, tender act.
Once, a boy crawled under a sheet,
touched the moist part, carried
the beautiful scent, a secret animal
on his finger all day.

An Insect Trapped in a White Bulb

is a tired image, unless
you take the insect to be
our minds. A flash will hold
an only breath over our streets
and houses, then release it
in a black whisper.
The filament of hope withers.
So I found a woman
in an American city
noted for its hybrid-French cuisine
and liberal liquor laws.
Nights, she becomes the cool pond
I am baptised in, held down
interminably by the shadow of God,
or just a shadow. Actually,
I have seen God
but only in women's eyes.
Once, on the smooth clipped green
of a golf course in Southern California,
too drunk to say anything but yes,
and again, yes, a girl opened
her diary to me and I erased
whole chapters. Afterward,
she wept and spoke of her father—
with an anger that dwarfed me
and everything I'd done to her—
through clenched teeth, spitting
his name, glaring over my shoulder,
on her back, beyond the clouds,
the stars. But before that even,
as an adolescent in Japan,

on a field trip to Nagasaki
where, at ground zero,
the stopped clocks,
glossies of human gargoyles
and clumps of melted coins
are kept in cases under glass,
I saw among the students
and the tourists, an old woman
in red kimono, hands pressed palm
to palm, the pupils of her eyes
rolled back so only the pinkish whites
glared out. *When the tissue is pierced*
the blood of prophets will spill through.
A sister to my gentler self
said this in a dream.
What frightens me is that if I phoned her now
she would understand. She would whisper
Richard, look at your hands,
they are the mask the merciful must wear
when the angels come,
and they are the frank gesture
we must make to the spirits
when we burn piñon . . . Richard,
when you hear the sirens
go to your windows and make a cross
in the air, spit into your hands,
turn three times and swallow a penny.
I held her once and listened
and listened.
She laughed and wept by turns
she changed by turns

from skinless flank
of ivory-colored meat
to shaft of smoky light,
and spoke till dawn of Armageddon
till I said *shshshshsh*.
At the train station,
leaning on a single silver crutch,
she said nothing. Many nights
from different cities
I've stared out of windows, thought,
Now, right this second, I'm ready.
Always, from the throes of that sentiment,
I am snapped back by the memory
of a grade-school film on insects.
It was about their ability to survive.
The last frame, over which the credits drifted
to a lively tune, was of the pink,
polyocular eyes of a bloated queen bee,
covering the entire screen.

Star Boys

All the tough dudes
are whistling in the dark.
Wildman Bob's in Chino.
Dirty Dave's doing time
in his daddy's garage.
Wolf's a woman.
Lizard's got nobody.
Now we all know nothing
really happens, boys.
Things just get perpetrated.
Besides, the sun's a pain
when you're tripping
on what's gone down
and I'd rather stick
my finger in the cool moon.
I'd rather sit and watch
purple curls of smoke
flatten on the ceiling
in the blacklite
chew on salted scallions
pop a couple beers
and think a white wall
till fog comes in early morning
and I can go outside
walk down to the pier
and listen to the birds
and water. But I can't
wait. The stars
are whistling lips
of the dead arranged

in a great tattoo and if
we could back up, boys,
I mean, right out of the universe,
we'd see it's just an anchor,
a naked body, a pierced heart.

Where Sparks Go

when they're spent
is where you are. So be
smart and gather them up;
they are the currency
of the unborn. Then step
forward into the bent
light of rage. It is there
you will put on gender.
Daughter, wise as weather,
intractable as I,
lucid as your mother:
I dream you such as this.
A tree I cannot name
is grunting into bloom.
The vagrant morning birds
are much more numerous.
A fresh season's old tune
is whistling down my spine
out of the protracted
dark of your solitude.
A young man should never
trust the easy wisdom
that preys upon him, yet
I am fast giving in
to accepting evil
as real and uncontested.
So why then do I feel
you are all around me,
insisting otherwise,
as though the inverse sum
of being were more than

words ever fix into
the syntax of passion?
As if what I would know
of the pain of others
is spurious and vague.
But a true image is
a rough drug. To put this
down as if for you who
will inherit nothing
is neither blind faith nor
a rank naiveté.
A confession, perhaps;
perhaps a little rank.
Do not be offended.
I stood once on a hill
overlooking the looped
intersection of four
freeways, and as the lights
snapped on, randomly as
stars, I was offended.
A friend, beautiful, dark,
shivered three miles away
in the *Tia Juana*
Clinic, a child inside
her choking
on salt. Two years after,
one starry summer morning,
she phoned me and said, *if
it had been a boy, what
would his name have been, if
it had been a girl . . .* if

pigs are taking over,
Daughter, I am a pig
with visionary
tendencies. I am
not taking over. I am
selling my hindquarters
to the One True Butcher
for a little chump change.
I love you where you are.
Behind your mother's breath,
among the long, wet sobs
that linger there, thinking
your name over and again
as you twirl a forelock
round a finger, you sit
muttering or humming,
striking a somber wish
against an old wet stone.

The Conch's Pink Swirl

to its center of dark,
a man unfolding his father's
blue shirt and the sky
making change on the water
come all into this picture
of dusk. Below the waves
there is a computer
in an iron vault and putting
on the shirt as the world's
light recedes, the man
notices a glimmer, like a candle
flicker under skin, from the shell
at his feet. Of course
it is the key to the iron vault.
We watch him walk toward
the water, changed. His hair,
for one thing, is on fire
but not smoking, and when
I touch your knee he turns—
his eyes glow red and clouds
peel over the last thread of sunset.
What if he is really my father
and what if the shirt he wears
is a legacy of sorrow and what if
I hold you close for an hour
and fuck all memory and bad weather.

About the Book

The text and display type are Optima. Composition and typesetting were done by G & S Typesetters of Austin, Texas. The book was printed on 60 lb. Warren's Olde Style paper and bound in Holliston Roxite by Kingsport Press, Kingsport, Tennessee.

Design and production were by Joyce Kachergis Book Design and Production, Bynum, North Carolina.

About the Author

"Movement" is central to *Green Dragons* and to its author, movement from one place to another and one life to another. Richard Katrovas passed much of his childhood in cars and motels with his parents and four younger siblings. His mother taught him to read in the back seat of a car. Later his father was sent to prison, his mother died, and he was adopted. He moved with his second family to Sasebo, Japan and then to San Diego.

Katrovas studied at San Diego State University (B.A., 1977), the University of Arkansas, the University of Virginia (Henry Hoyns Fellow 1979–80), and the University of Iowa, from which he received his M.F.A. in 1983. He addresses most of his poems to people he has known, out of a commitment to "recognizing the interpenetration of the inner life and the world of others," as well as to recognizing his own "simmering rage which I don't understand, but I know I share with others." He finds through his work an "inexplicable redemption."

Katrovas teaches at the University of New Orleans. His poems have appeared in *Antioch Review, Crazy Horse, The Missouri Review, North American Review*, and other magazines.